Beyond Me
The Leader's Guide
to Team Excellence

Kenneth S. Roberts

Copyright Message

Introduction

Beyond Me – The Journey to Team Excellence

In today's dynamic business landscape, leaders are confronted with a pervasive challenge that transcends traditional paradigms – the struggle to foster a culture of true collaboration and unleash the full potential of their teams. This challenge, often masked by organizational silos, communication breakdowns, and a lack of genuine engagement, demands a transformative solution.

In the heart of this challenge lies the intricate labyrinth of team dynamics. Leaders grapple with the complexities of balancing individual aspirations with collective goals, and the elusive quest for team excellence becomes a daunting task. Autocratic approaches stifle creativity, charismatic visions sometimes falter in execution, and the traditional leadership playbook falls short in guiding leaders through the nuanced landscape of team-centric leadership.

Enter "Beyond Me," a beacon of light amidst the complexity. This book transcends the conventional leadership discourse, offering insights, narratives, and principles that illuminate the path to team excellence. It's not just a guide; it's your compass, navigating you through the intricacies of prioritizing team needs, fostering active listening, and cultivating a culture where collaboration thrives.

Now, as you stand at the intersection of challenge and solution, "Beyond Me" extends a compelling call to action. Are you ready to step beyond the limitations of traditional leadership? Will you embrace the principles within these pages to transform your team dynamics? The journey awaits, and the destination is team excellence – a place where the collective brilliance of your team becomes the driving force behind lasting success.

Embark on this transformative journey, unlock the full potential of your team, and redefine your leadership narrative. "Beyond Me" is not just a book; it's an invitation to lead with resilience, authenticity, and a profound understanding of the power inherent in collaborative leadership. The voyage begins now. Are you ready to go beyond?

CHAPTER ONE

Team-Centric Leadership: Embracing a Collaborative Paradigm

Defining Team-Centric Leadership

In the ever-evolving landscape of leadership, the notion of Team-Centric Leadership has emerged as a transformative paradigm that places emphasis on collaboration, shared decision-making, and the collective strength of a team. Unlike traditional hierarchical models, Team-Centric Leadership sees leaders not as sole decision-makers but as facilitators of a collaborative process where the team's collective intelligence is harnessed for organizational success. This approach recognizes that a team, when empowered and aligned, can achieve outcomes that surpass individual contributions.

The Evolution of Leadership Styles

The evolution of leadership styles reflects broader shifts in organizational culture and workplace dynamics. From autocratic models where leaders wielded unquestionable authority to more democratic approaches that sought input from team members, the trajectory has been towards greater inclusivity. Team-Centric Leadership marks the pinnacle of this evolution, acknowledging that the complexity of modern challenges demands a collective and diverse approach. This chapter delves into the roots of Team-Centric Leadership, tracing its evolution and highlighting the need for a leadership style that aligns with the dynamics of the contemporary professional landscape.

The Impact of Team-Centric Leadership on Organizational Culture

Organizational culture is the bedrock upon which successful teams are built. Team-Centric Leadership serves as a catalyst for cultivating a culture that values collaboration, open communication, and mutual respect. The impact of Team-Centric Leadership on organizational culture is profound—it nurtures an environment where each team member's strengths are recognized, ideas are welcomed, and decision-making becomes a shared responsibility. This section explores how Team-Centric Leadership becomes a driving force for shaping a positive and inclusive culture that not only enhances team performance but also contributes to the overall success and sustainability of the organization.

As we embark on an exploration of Team-Centric Leadership, it becomes evident that this approach goes beyond mere delegation; it represents a fundamental shift in the philosophy of leadership. It acknowledges that the strength of a leader lies not just in individual capabilities but in the ability to harness the collective power of a team. The ensuing sections will dissect key components of Team-Centric Leadership, emphasizing the prioritization of team needs in decision-making and the art of fostering active listening—an essential skill that serves as the linchpin for effective collaboration within a team-centric framework.

Prioritizing Team Needs in Decision-Making: Understanding the Essence

Understanding Team Dynamics

1. Team Composition and Diversity

The foundation of prioritizing team needs lies in recognizing the multifaceted nature of team composition. Diverse skill sets, backgrounds, and perspectives within a team contribute to its collective intelligence. Sustainable team-centric leaders appreciate the inherent strength in diversity and intentionally build teams with complementary skills. This section explores the strategic considerations involved in team composition and the importance of fostering an inclusive environment where every team member feels valued and contributes uniquely to the team's success.

2. Roles and Responsibilities

Prioritizing team needs involves the strategic allocation of roles and responsibilities. Effective teams function like well-oiled machines, with each member understanding their role in achieving common goals. Sustainable team-centric leaders excel in defining clear roles and responsibilities, ensuring a balanced distribution of tasks, and fostering an environment where every team member's contribution is integral to the team's success. This section examines the art of role assignment and how it contributes to a harmonious and high-performing team.

Team Empowerment in Decision-Making

1. Inclusive Decision-Making Processes

Team-centric leaders understand that decision-making is a collective endeavor. Inclusive decision-making processes go beyond soliciting input; they actively engage team members in shaping decisions that impact the entire team. This involves creating a culture where diverse opinions are not only welcomed but considered essential for robust decision-making. The section explores methodologies for inclusive decision-making and strategies to foster a collaborative decision-making culture within teams.

2. Balancing Autonomy and Guidance

Empowering teams requires striking a delicate balance between granting autonomy and providing guidance. Successful team-centric leaders recognize that autonomy fuels creativity and innovation, but guidance ensures alignment with organizational objectives. This section delves into the art of balancing autonomy, allowing teams the freedom to explore ideas while maintaining a strategic framework that aligns with broader organizational goals. It explores how the interplay of autonomy and guidance contributes to a team-centric decision-making process.

Cultivating a Culture of Trust

1. Building Trust within Teams

Trust is the bedrock of effective team dynamics. Prioritizing team needs involves cultivating a culture of trust where team members feel safe to express ideas, voice concerns, and challenge the status quo. Team-centric leaders invest in building trust through transparent communication, consistent actions, and a commitment to fostering an environment where trust thrives. This section explores actionable strategies for building and maintaining trust within teams.

2. Transparency in Decision-Making

Transparency in decision-making is a key element of prioritizing team needs. Team-centric leaders communicate openly about the decision-making process, providing insights into the rationale behind choices and involving the team in understanding the broader context. Transparent leadership fosters a sense of inclusion and helps team members see their role in the larger organizational picture. This section examines how transparency contributes to a culture of trust and shared responsibility within teams.

As we delve into the nuances of prioritizing team needs in decision-making, it becomes clear that this approach is not a mere checkbox on a leadership checklist. It represents a fundamental shift in the way decisions are approached—shifting from individual to collective, from hierarchical to inclusive. Sustainable team-centric leaders recognize that decisions made with a focus on the team's needs have a ripple effect, fostering a collaborative and resilient team culture that propels the organization towards sustained success.

Fostering Active Listening as a Leader: Engaging the Heart of Collaboration

Foundations of Active Listening

1. The Importance of Active Listening

At the heart of team-centric leadership lies the profound skill of active listening. Recognizing the importance of active listening is pivotal for leaders seeking to foster collaboration within their teams. This section explores how active listening transcends mere hearing, delving into its transformative impact on team communication, trust-building, and overall cohesion. Team-centric leaders understand that active listening is not just a technique but a fundamental element of empathetic and effective leadership.

2. Non-Verbal Cues and Body Language

Active listening extends beyond verbal communication to encompass non-verbal cues and body language. Team-centric leaders adeptly read between the lines, understanding the emotions, concerns, and unspoken thoughts of their team members. This section unravels the art of interpreting non-verbal cues, emphasizing the role of body language in building rapport and creating an environment where team members feel truly heard.

Effective Communication Strategies

1. Clarity and Conciseness

Active listening is complemented by the leader's ability to communicate with clarity and conciseness. Clear and concise communication ensures that team members receive messages accurately, minimizing misunderstandings. Team-centric leaders master the art of conveying complex ideas in a straightforward manner, fostering an environment where everyone, regardless of their role or background, can comprehend and contribute effectively.

2. Questioning Techniques

A key component of active listening is the skillful use of questioning techniques.

Team-centric leaders employ insightful questions to encourage team members to express their thoughts, share perspectives, and contribute meaningfully to discussions. This section delves into the various questioning strategies that leaders can employ to stimulate thoughtful dialogue, uncover hidden insights, and create an inclusive space for team members.

Emotional Intelligence in Listening

1. Empathy and Understanding

Empathy is the cornerstone of active listening in team-centric leadership. Leaders with high emotional intelligence connect on a deeper level with their team members, understanding not just the words spoken but the emotions behind them. This section explores how cultivating empathy fosters a culture of understanding and compassion, contributing to stronger relationships and a more cohesive team.

2. Managing Conflicts Through Listening

Active listening becomes a powerful tool in managing conflicts within a team. Team-centric leaders approach conflicts with the intention of understanding divergent viewpoints. They listen actively to the concerns and grievances of team members, transforming conflicts into opportunities for growth and resolution. This section provides practical strategies for leveraging active listening to navigate conflicts effectively and maintain a harmonious team environment.

As we navigate the intricate landscape of fostering active listening as a leader, it becomes evident that this skill is not just a communication tactic—it is the heartbeat of team-centric leadership. Leaders who prioritize active listening lay the groundwork for a team culture characterized by openness, understanding, and collaborative problem-solving. The subsequent sections will tie together the threads of prioritizing team needs and fostering active listening, illustrating how these two pillars synergize to create a team-centric leadership approach that propels organizations towards resilience, innovation, and sustained success.

Conclusion:
Nurturing a Team-Centric Leadership Culture

As we conclude this exploration into team-centric leadership, the synthesis of prioritizing team needs in decision-making and fostering active listening emerges as a potent formula for nurturing a culture of collaboration and cohesion within organizations. This dynamic approach to leadership transcends traditional models, positioning the team as the focal point for success.

The Long-Term Impact of Prioritizing Team Needs and Fostering Active Listening

The long-term impact of prioritizing team needs in decision-making and fostering active listening is profound. Organizations led by team-centric principles experience enhanced adaptability, innovation, and resilience. By valuing the diverse contributions of team members and creating an inclusive decision-making environment, leaders foster a sense of ownership and commitment. Active listening becomes the cornerstone of transparent communication, building trust and strengthening the bonds that hold the team together.

The ripple effect extends beyond the team itself—organizations that prioritize team-centric leadership witness improved employee engagement, increased productivity, and heightened overall satisfaction. The collaborative spirit cultivated through active listening and inclusive decision-making permeates the organizational culture, shaping it into one that thrives on creativity, empathy, and shared goals.

Encouraging the Adoption of Team-Centric Leadership Practices

Encouraging the adoption of team-centric leadership practices involves a cultural shift within organizations. Leaders play a pivotal role in setting the tone and modeling the behavior they wish to see. By showcasing the benefits of prioritizing team needs and fostering active listening, leaders inspire others to embrace this approach. Training programs, mentorship initiatives, and continuous communication about the positive outcomes of team-centric leadership further solidify its integration into the organizational DNA.

As organizations embark on this journey towards a team-centric leadership culture, they position themselves not only for immediate success but for sustained excellence. This approach aligns seamlessly with the demands of a dynamic and interconnected world, where collaborative innovation and a responsive organizational culture are key differentiators.

In essence, team-centric leadership is not a destination but a continuous journey of growth and adaptation. It requires leaders to be perpetual learners, open to feedback, and committed to the ongoing development of their teams. The practices explored in this chapter serve as guideposts for leaders seeking to navigate this journey, fostering an environment where teams flourish, individuals thrive, and organizations achieve enduring success.

In the evolving landscape of leadership, team-centric principles stand as a testament to the collective strength of a united team. As organizations embrace this ethos, they not only elevate their team dynamics but also contribute to a broader narrative of leadership that champions collaboration, inclusivity, and sustainable success.

CHAPTER 2

Promoting Collaborative Culture

In the dynamic landscape of modern workplaces, fostering a collaborative culture has become a critical aspect of organizational success. This chapter delves into key strategies for promoting collaboration within teams, departments, and across the entire organization. By breaking down departmental silos, facilitating transparent communication, and utilizing effective team-building initiatives, organizations can cultivate an environment where collaboration thrives, leading to innovation, improved productivity, and overall success.

Breaking Down Departmental Silos

Understanding Silos in Organizations

In many organizations, the term "silo" refers to the isolated nature of individual departments or teams. Silos emerge when departments become insular, focusing solely on their specific tasks and goals without adequate communication or collaboration with other parts of the organization. This isolation can lead to redundancy, lack of innovation, and an overall reduction in organizational efficiency.

Recognizing silos is crucial, as they often manifest as invisible barriers that hinder the free flow of information and ideas. Employees within siloed departments may not be aware of the broader organizational goals, leading to a disconnect between the department's activities and the overall mission.

Identifying Silo Factors

Several factors contribute to the formation and persistence of silos within organizations. These may include:

- Lack of Communication Channels: When there's a dearth of effective communication channels between departments, information tends to stay confined within each silo
- Conflicting Goals: Departments may have conflicting or divergent goals, leading to a competitive rather than collaborative environment.
- Hierarchical Structures: Rigid hierarchical structures can reinforce silos by limiting the flow of information between different levels of the organization.
- Inadequate Leadership: Leaders who do not actively encourage collaboration or fail to address silo-forming behaviors contribute to their persistence.

Understanding these factors is crucial for leadership, as it forms the foundation for dismantling silos effectively.

Leadership's Role in Silo Breaking

Leadership plays a pivotal role in breaking down departmental silos. Leaders must foster a culture of collaboration and shared objectives. Key actions include:

- Encouraging Collaboration: Leaders should actively promote collaboration by emphasizing shared goals and the interconnectedness of different departments.
- Creating Cross-Functional Teams: Breaking down silos often involves creating cross-functional teams that bring together members from various departments to work on specific projects. This breaks down the "us versus them" mentality.

- Aligning Goals: Leaders need to ensure that the goals of each department align with the broader organizational mission. This alignment helps in creating a unified sense of purpose.

Leadership should actively communicate the importance of collaboration and provide the necessary resources to support initiatives aimed at dismantling silos.

Promoting Cross-Departmental Collaboration
To promote collaboration between departments, organizations can implement several practical strategies:

- Cross-Departmental Meetings: Regular meetings involving representatives from different departments can facilitate the exchange of information and ideas. These meetings provide a platform for understanding the challenges faced by each department and finding common ground.

- Joint Projects: Encouraging departments to collaborate on projects can foster teamwork and break down silos. Working towards a common goal encourages communication and shared problem-solving.
- Shared Metrics and KPIs: Establishing shared key performance indicators (KPIs) that align with organizational goals promotes a sense of shared responsibility. Departments are more likely to collaborate when their success is tied to collective achievemen
- Cultivating a Collaborative Culture: Creating a culture that values collaboration is essential. Recognition and rewards for collaborative efforts can incentivize departments to work together.
- Technology Integration: Leveraging technology can be instrumental in breaking down silos. Implementing collaboration tools, project management software, and communication platforms can facilitate real-time information

sharing. These tools create a centralized hub where teams from different departments can collaborate seamlessly, diminishing the barriers created by physical separation.

- Training and Development Programs: Investing in training programs that emphasize collaboration skills is essential. These programs can include workshops on effective communication, conflict resolution, and team-building exercises. By enhancing employees' ability to work collaboratively, organizations can break down the silo mentality.

- Encouraging Employee Rotation: Facilitating opportunities for employees to rotate between departments fosters cross-functional understanding. When individuals experience working in different parts of the organization, they gain a broader perspective and develop relationships that transcend departmental boundaries.

- Open Communication Platforms: Establishing open communication platforms, such as company-wide forums or intranet systems, provides a space for employees to share insights, updates, and challenges. This transparency helps break down information silos and creates a culture of openness and inclusivity.

Conclusion

Breaking down departmental silos is an ongoing process that requires a multi-faceted approach. By understanding the factors contributing to silos, leadership can actively work to reshape the organizational culture. Encouraging collaboration, creating cross-functional teams, aligning goals, and implementing technology solutions are essential steps in this journey. Ultimately, the goal is to create an organizational environment where information flows freely, and teams collaborate seamlessly to achieve common objectives. The subsequent sections will delve into additional strategies for fostering collaboration, with a focus on transparent communication and effective team-building initiatives.

Promoting cross-departmental collaboration requires a concerted effort to remove structural and cultural barriers, fostering an environment where information and ideas can flow freely between different parts of the organization. This approach not only improves overall organizational effectiveness but also enhances the satisfaction and engagement of employees who feel a sense of purpose and unity with their colleagues across departments.

Facilitating Transparent Communication

The Importance of Transparent Communication

Transparent communication serves as the cornerstone of a collaborative culture. It involves sharing information openly, honestly, and consistently throughout the organization. This practice builds trust among team members and helps align everyone with the organization's goals, fostering a sense of unity and shared purpose.

Creating Open Channels

Establishing open communication channels is vital for transparency. This involves selecting appropriate platforms for communication, such as intranet systems, collaboration tools, and regular town hall meetings. The goal is to provide avenues for information flow that are accessible to all team members, irrespective of their position within the organization.

- Intranet Systems: Utilize internal networks where information, updates, and announcements can be centralized. This provides a go-to place for employees to access important information, fostering a sense of transparency.
- Collaboration Tools: Implement tools like project management software or communication platforms that allow

real-time collaboration. These tools not only enhance communication but also provide visibility into ongoing projects, promoting transparency.

- Regular Town Hall Meetings: Hold periodic town hall meetings where leadership communicates openly with the entire organization. This platform allows for the dissemination of important updates, strategy discussions, and an opportunity for employees to ask questions or share concerns.

Encouraging Honest Feedback

Transparent communication is a two-way street, requiring active participation from both leaders and team members. Leaders should create an environment where team members feel encouraged to provide honest feedback without fear of reprisal.

- Active Listening: Leaders should actively listen to the concerns, suggestions, and ideas of their team. This involves giving full attention, asking clarifying questions, and demonstrating a genuine interest in understanding different perspectives.

- Constructive Criticism:** Foster a culture where constructive criticism is viewed as a tool for improvement. Encourage team members to provide feedback in a way that is constructive, specific, and geared towards finding solutions.

- Recognition of Diverse Perspectives:** Acknowledge and appreciate the diversity of thought within the organization. Transparent communication embraces the understanding that different team members bring unique perspectives, and valuing this diversity contributes to a rich and innovative work environment.

Addressing Communication Challenges

Transparent communication faces various challenges, and organizations must actively work to overcome them to ensure a truly collaborative culture.

- Language Barriers: In a globalized workforce, language differences can pose a challenge. Providing language training, utilizing translation tools, and promoting clear and concise communication can help bridge these gaps.
- Remote Work Challenges: With the rise of remote work, organizations must find ways to maintain transparent communication. This involves leveraging virtual communication tools, scheduling regular video conferences, and fostering a sense of connection among remote team members.
- Generational Differences: Different generations within the workforce may have varying communication preferences. A transparent communication strategy should consider these differences and incorporate diverse methods, such as combining digital communication with in-person meetings.

By addressing these aspects of transparent communication, organizations can cultivate an environment where information flows freely, feedback is encouraged, and challenges in communication are proactively tackled. This sets the stage for a collaborative culture where everyone feels informed, engaged, and empowered to contribute to the organization's success.

Utilizing Team-Building Initiatives

The Essence of Team Building

Team building is not just a set of activities; it's a strategic approach to enhancing collaboration and cohesion among team members. The essence lies in creating an environment where individuals can build trust, understand each other's strengths and weaknesses, and collectively work towards shared goals.

- Trust-Building Exercises: Incorporate activities that foster trust among team members. Trust is the foundation of collaboration, and team-building initiatives should provide opportunities for individuals to rely on each other, share vulnerabilities, and develop a sense of trust.

- Strengths Assessment: Utilize strengths assessments to identify the unique skills and talents of team members. Understanding each other's strengths enables better collaboration, as tasks can be assigned based on individual expertise, leading to a more effective and harmonious team.

Designing Tailored Team Building Activities

Not all team-building activities are one-size-fits-all. Tailor initiatives to address specific challenges within the organization, ensuring that they align with the organizational culture and objectives.

- Customized Workshops: Organize workshops that specifically address the needs and challenges faced by the team.

Whether it's improving communication, resolving conflicts, or enhancing creativity, tailor the content to directly benefit the team's dynamics.

- Contextual Team Challenges: Design challenges that mirror real-world scenarios the team might encounter. This not only makes the activities more engaging but also ensures that the skills developed during these challenges are directly applicable to the team's work environment.

Incorporating Fun and Engagement

Team building doesn't have to be a serious affair; in fact, injecting elements of fun and engagement is crucial for its success.

- Interactive Games: Include interactive games that encourage laughter, creativity, and spontaneity. These games break down barriers, build camaraderie, and contribute to an overall positive team spirit.

- Team-Building Retreats: Consider organizing team-building retreats in an informal setting. These events provide an opportunity for team members to relax, bond, and engage in activities outside the usual work environment, fostering a sense of camaraderie.

Sustaining Team Building Results

The impact of team building shouldn't be ephemeral. Organizations must implement strategies to ensure that the positive outcomes are sustained over the long term.

- Integration into Daily Work: Infuse the principles and lessons learned from team-building activities into daily work. This might involve incorporating specific communication techniques, problem-solving approaches, or collaborative strategies into routine tasks.

- Regular Check-ins: Schedule regular check-ins or follow-up sessions to assess the ongoing impact of team-building initiatives. These sessions provide an opportunity for team members to reflect on their experiences, share insights, and discuss how the lessons learned are being applied in their work.

Conclusion:

Promoting a collaborative culture through transparent communication and effective team-building initiatives is a continuous process that requires commitment from leadership and active participation from every team member. By breaking down departmental silos, fostering transparent communication, and engaging in purposeful team-building activities, organizations can create an environment where collaboration thrives.

In the interconnected and rapidly changing landscape of modern workplaces, organizations that prioritize collaboration are better equipped to adapt, innovate, and succeed. A collaborative culture not only enhances individual and team performance but also contributes to the overall resilience and sustainability of the organization in an ever-evolving business landscape.

CHAPTER 3

Emotional Intelligence in Action

In the realm of leadership and interpersonal relationships, emotional intelligence (EI) stands as a pivotal skill. This chapter explores the practical application of emotional intelligence in various facets of professional and personal life. By delving into the nuanced components of EI—acknowledging and validating emotions, fostering inclusive communication, and embracing diversity and inclusion—we uncover how emotional intelligence transforms relationships, teams, and organizational cultures.

Certainly! Let's delve deeper into the points under "Understanding and Validating Emotions" in the context of Emotional Intelligence (EI) in action:

Understanding and Validating Emotions

Understanding Emotional Intelligence:
Emotional intelligence (EI) encompasses a range of skills that collectively contribute to effective emotional management and interpersonal relationships. These skills include:

- Self-awareness: It involves the capacity to identify and comprehend one's own emotions. This involves being in tune with feelings, identifying triggers, and understanding how emotions impact behavior.
- Self-Regulation: The capacity to manage and control one's emotions, preventing impulsive reactions. It involves staying calm under pressure, adapting to changing circumstances, and handling stress effectively.
- Empathy: The capacity to identify and comprehend the feelings of other people. Empathetic individuals can put themselves in someone else's shoes, which is crucial

for building strong interpersonal connections.

- Motivation: Internal motivation that drives individuals to pursue goals with passion and resilience. Emotionally intelligent individuals are often self-motivated, deriving satisfaction from their work and maintaining a positive outlook.
- Social skills: It encompass the proficiency to navigate social situations with effectiveness. This includes communication, conflict resolution, and the capacity to build and maintain relationships.

The Power of Acknowledging Emotions

Acknowledging emotions, both one's own and those of others, is the foundational step in developing emotional intelligence. This involves:

- Self-Awareness in Action: Recognizing and accepting one's emotions without judgment. Acknowledging feelings allows individuals to better understand their motivations, reactions, and decision-making processes.

- Empathy in Practice: Acknowledging the emotions of others by actively listening and perceiving non-verbal cues. This creates a supportive environment and fosters meaningful connections.
- Promoting Emotional Literacy: Encouraging individuals to label and articulate their emotions. This enhances emotional literacy, enabling clearer communication and a deeper understanding of personal and collective emotional experiences.

Validating Emotions for Connection

Validation goes beyond mere acknowledgment; it involves expressing understanding and empathy towards someone's emotional experience. This contributes to creating authentic connections and positive relationships:

- Active Listening as Validation: Actively listening to someone's emotions without judgment or interruption. This involves paraphrasing, summarizing, and reflecting back what has been shared, demonstrating genuine interest and concern.
- Expressing Empathy: Communicating empathy by acknowledging the validity of another person's emotions. This involves validating their experiences, even if perspectives differ, and showing compassion towards their feelings.
- Creating a Safe Space: Establishing an environment where individuals feel safe to express their emotions. This involves leaders and team members creating a culture that encourages open communication and values the emotional well-being of everyone.

Practical Strategies for Acknowledgment and Validation

Offering specific strategies to implement acknowledgment and validation in daily interactions:

- Regular Self-Reflection: Encouraging individuals to engage in regular self-reflection to understand their emotional responses and patterns. This can be facilitated through journaling or mindfulness practices.
- Empathy-building Exercises: Providing exercises or scenarios that promote the development of empathy. This can include role-playing, case studies, or team activities that require individuals to consider different emotional perspectives.
- Training Programs: Implementing emotional intelligence training programs within organizations. These programs can provide tools and techniques for understanding and validating emotions,

enhancing interpersonal skills, and fostering a positive emotional climate.

By incorporating these aspects into the understanding and validation of emotions, individuals and organizations can lay the groundwork for a more emotionally intelligent and connected environment. These practices contribute to enhanced communication, strengthened relationships, and a positive emotional culture within teams and organizations.

Fostering Inclusive Communication

The Intersection of Emotional Intelligence and Inclusion

Understanding the intersection between emotional intelligence and inclusion is crucial for creating a workplace where diverse perspectives are valued. This involves:

- Cultural Awareness: Developing cultural intelligence and awareness of diverse perspectives. Emotionally intelligent individuals recognize the impact of cultural differences on communication and proactively seek to understand and respect these nuances.

- Inclusive Leadership: Acknowledging the role of leaders in fostering inclusive communication. Emotionally intelligent leaders actively create an environment where every team member feels heard, valued, and included, regardless of their background or identity.

Creating a Culture of Open Dialogue:
Fostering a culture of open dialogue involves cultivating an environment where individuals feel comfortable expressing their thoughts, ideas, and concerns. This includes:

- Psychological Safety: Recognizing the importance of psychological safety in encouraging open communication. Emotionally intelligent leaders create an atmosphere where individuals feel secure expressing diverse opinions without fear of retribution.

- Leadership Tone-Setting: The role of leadership in setting the tone for open dialogue. Emotionally intelligent leaders model transparent communication, vulnerability, and a willingness to engage in constructive conversations.

Conflict Resolution Through Emotional Intelligence

Emotional intelligence plays a pivotal role in conflict resolution within diverse teams. This includes:

- Empathy in Conflict Resolution: Applying empathy to understand different perspectives during conflicts. Emotionally intelligent individuals actively listen, seek to comprehend the underlying emotions, and work towards solutions that consider the feelings of all parties involved.

- Constructive Communication: Promoting constructive communication during conflicts. This involves avoiding blame, focusing on the issue at hand, and using emotional intelligence to navigate potentially sensitive conversations without escalating tensions.

Practical Strategies for Inclusive Communication

Offering practical strategies to foster inclusive communication within organizations:

- Diversity Training: Implementing diversity and inclusion training programs. These programs can educate individuals on cultural competence, unconscious bias, and effective communication strategies in diverse settings.

- Inclusive Language Guidelines: Establishing guidelines for inclusive language. This involves promoting language that respects and values individuals regardless of their background, ensuring that communication is inclusive and free from unintentional biases.

- Diverse Perspectives Platforms: Creating platforms or forums for individuals to share diverse perspectives. This can include discussion groups, mentorship programs, or initiatives that actively seek input from individuals with varying backgrounds and experiences.

Measuring and Sustaining Inclusive Communication Growth

Measuring progress and ensuring sustainability in fostering inclusive communication involves:

- Feedback Mechanisms: Implementing regular feedback mechanisms to assess the inclusivity of communication practices. Emotionally intelligent organizations actively seek input from employees to understand their experiences and perceptions.

- Inclusion Metrics: Establishing metrics to measure the inclusivity of communication strategies. This can involve tracking participation rates in diversity programs, monitoring employee satisfaction with communication channels, and assessing the representation of diverse voices in decision-making processes.

By incorporating these elements into the fostering of inclusive communication, organizations can create a workplace where every individual feels valued, heard, and included. Emotionally intelligent leaders play a key role in shaping a culture that actively embraces diverse perspectives and fosters open dialogue, contributing to a more inclusive and collaborative work environment.

Embracing Diversity and Inclusion:

Diversity as a Catalyst for Emotional Intelligence

Recognizing diversity as a catalyst for developing emotional intelligence involves understanding how exposure to diverse perspectives enhances empathy, cultural awareness, and overall emotional intelligence. Key aspects include:

- Cultural Intelligence: Emphasizing the development of cultural intelligence to navigate diverse environments. This involves being curious about and appreciative of different cultures, customs, and communication styles.
- Cognitive Diversity: Acknowledging the value of cognitive diversity in problem-solving. Emotionally intelligent individuals recognize that diverse perspectives contribute to innovative solutions and creative thinking.

Cultivating an Inclusive Mindset

Cultivating an inclusive mindset through emotional intelligence involves actively challenging biases, appreciating differences, and fostering an environment where every individual feels a sense of belonging. This includes:

- Bias Awareness: Promoting awareness of unconscious biases and providing tools to mitigate their impact. Emotionally intelligent individuals actively work to recognize and address their own biases, creating a more inclusive atmosphere.

- Inclusive Language: Encouraging the use of inclusive language that respects individual identities and backgrounds. Emotionally intelligent communication involves avoiding stereotypes and embracing language that values diversity.

Practical Strategies for Inclusivity

Providing practical strategies to actively promote diversity and inclusion within organizations:

- Diverse Hiring Practices: Implementing inclusive hiring practices that consider a broad range of qualifications and experiences. Emotionally intelligent organizations actively seek diversity in their talent pool and work to eliminate biases in recruitment processes.

- Employee Resource Groups: Establishing Employee Resource Groups (ERGs) to provide support and community for individuals from diverse backgrounds. These groups foster a sense of belonging and create platforms for sharing experiences and insights.

- Inclusive Policies: Developing and enforcing policies that actively promote diversity and inclusion. This can include flexible work arrangements, accommodation for diverse needs, and a commitment to equal opportunities for career advancement.

Measuring and Sustaining Diversity and Inclusion Efforts

Measuring progress and ensuring sustainability in embracing diversity and inclusion involves:

- Diversity Metrics: Establishing measurable diversity metrics to track representation and inclusion efforts. This can include monitoring the diversity of the workforce, leadership positions, and participation in diversity programs.
- Inclusive Leadership Training: Providing training programs for leaders on inclusive leadership. Emotionally intelligent leaders actively engage in ongoing training to understand and address diversity challenges, creating a more inclusive organizational culture.
- Employee Feedback Surveys: Conducting regular employee feedback surveys to gauge the effectiveness of diversity and

inclusion initiatives. Emotionally intelligent organizations seek input from employees to continually improve and adapt their strategies.

By incorporating these elements into the embrace of diversity and inclusion, organizations can move beyond mere acknowledgment to actively fostering a culture where every individual feels valued and included. Emotional intelligence serves as a guiding force in creating an environment that celebrates diversity, promotes inclusivity, and enhances the overall well-being and performance of the entire organization.

Conclusion

In conclusion, embracing diversity and inclusion through the lens of emotional intelligence is not just a strategic initiative; it's a transformative commitment that reshapes organizational culture and elevates individual and collective emotional intelligence. By recognizing diversity as a catalyst for emotional intelligence, cultivating an inclusive mindset, and implementing practical strategies, organizations can create environments where individuals of diverse backgrounds thrive.

The intersection of emotional intelligence and inclusion highlights the profound impact leaders can have. Leaders with high emotional intelligence actively champion diversity, challenge biases, and foster a culture where every voice is not only heard but valued. This inclusive leadership sets the tone for open dialogue, conflict resolution, and a workplace where individuals can bring their authentic selves to work.

Measuring and sustaining diversity and inclusion efforts is essential for long-term success. Establishing diversity metrics, providing ongoing training, and actively seeking employee feedback ensure that organizations continually evolve and adapt to the changing dynamics of inclusivity. Emotionally intelligent leaders play a critical role in this process, creating an environment where diversity is not just a checkbox but an integral part of the organizational DNA.

In the evolving landscape of the modern workplace, where diversity is a strength and inclusion is a priority, emotional intelligence emerges as the guiding force that propels organizations toward success. It not only shapes how individuals understand and navigate their own emotions but also influences how they connect with others, resolve conflicts, and contribute to a culture of genuine acceptance and collaboration.

Embracing diversity and inclusion through the lens of emotional intelligence is a journey, not a destination. It's a commitment to continuous learning, introspection, and action. As organizations and leaders embrace this journey, they not only foster environments where individuals from all backgrounds can thrive but also contribute to a broader societal shift towards greater understanding, empathy, and collective well-being.

CHAPTER FOUR

Aligning Goals for Success

The alignment of goals within an organization is a pivotal factor in achieving sustained success. This chapter delves into the intricate process of aligning individual and team objectives with the overarching vision of the organization. By exploring key components such as clearly communicating team objectives, linking individual goals to the organizational vision, and reinforcing the collective vision, we unravel the essential strategies for creating a cohesive, purpose-driven, and high-performing team.

Clearly Communicating Team Objectives

Importance of Clarity in Communication
Clear communication is the bedrock of successful team collaboration and goal achievement. When team objectives are

communicated with precision and transparency, it minimizes misunderstandings, reduces confusion, and lays the foundation for a unified effort. Let's take a closer look at key[vital] aspects:

Clarity in Language

- Precision Matters: The language used to communicate team objectives must be precise and unambiguous. Ambiguity can lead to varied interpretations, potentially derailing efforts.

- Avoiding Jargon: Steer clear of industry-specific jargon that might be unclear to some team members. The goal is to ensure that everyone comprehends the objectives in the same way.

Utilizing Visual Aids

- Visualizing the Path Forward: Visual aids such as charts, diagrams, or project roadmaps are powerful tools. They provide a clear visual representation of the team's objectives, making complex information more accessible.

- Simplifying Complexity: In complex projects, visual aids simplify intricate details, enabling team members to grasp the overall direction and their individual roles.

Creating a Shared Understanding

Achieving clarity in communication extends beyond delivering information; it involves ensuring that every team member not only hears but truly understands the objectives. This involves:

Interactive Team Meetings

- Engagement and Participation: Team meetings should be interactive forums where team members actively engage in discussions about objectives. Encouraging questions and open dialogue promotes a shared understanding.
- Feedback Loops: Establishing feedback loops during meetings helps gauge

comprehension. Team leaders can actively seek input, ensuring that team members feel heard and clarifying any points of confusion.

Individual Goal Alignment

- Contextualizing Individual Contributions: Team members need to see the connection between their individual goals and the broader team objectives. Leaders play a pivotal role in articulating how each person's efforts contribute to the collective success.
- Aligning Personal Aspirations: Aligning individual goals with personal aspirations fosters a sense of purpose. When team members understand the impact of their work, motivation and commitment naturally follow.

Encouraging Questions and Feedback

- Fostering a Culture of Curiosity: Leaders should foster a culture where questions are not just permitted but encouraged. Team members should feel comfortable seeking clarification and providing feedback.

- Continuous Improvement: Actively using feedback for continuous improvement ensures that communication methods evolve to meet the team's changing needs. It creates a culture of adaptability and shared responsibility.

Measurement and Progress Tracking

To reinforce clarity and maintain focus, it's crucial to establish metrics for measuring progress toward team objectives. This involves:

Key Performance Indicators (KPIs)

- Defining Success Benchmarks: Identifying and clearly communicating key performance indicators (KPIs) sets benchmarks for success. Each team member should understand how their work contributes to achieving these indicators.
- Measuring Impact: Regularly measuring and sharing progress against KPIs

provides tangible evidence of how the team is moving towards its objectives.

Regular Progress Updates
- Transparent Communication: Transparently communicating successes and challenges maintains alignment. Regular progress updates, whether through meetings or communication channels, keep the team informed and motivated.
- Timely Adjustments: If obstacles arise, timely communication allows for adjustments. The team can collectively strategize on overcoming challenges, ensuring that deviations don't impede overall progress.

Effective communication of team objectives is not a one-time event but an ongoing process. It requires leaders to continuously refine their communication strategies, ensuring that clarity is maintained even as goals evolve and the team faces new challenges. In essence, clarity in communication sets the stage for a well-informed, engaged, and high-performing team.

Linking Individual Goals to Organizational Vision

Understanding the Organizational Vision

For individual goals to align effectively with the broader organizational vision, there must be a profound understanding of that vision at all levels of the team. This involves:

Leadership Communication

- Articulating the Vision:** Leaders play a pivotal role in clearly articulating the overarching vision of the organization. This communication should be consistent across various channels, including company-wide meetings, newsletters, and internal communications platforms.
- Inspiring Commitment:** The communication of the organizational vision should not just inform but inspire.

Leaders should convey the significance of the vision, helping team members connect emotionally to the broader purpose.

Connecting Values to Goals

- Alignment with Core Values:** Individual goals gain meaning when aligned with the core values and mission of the organization. Leaders must emphasize the connection between personal objectives and the organization's purpose.
- Enhancing Motivation: When team members see their work as contributing to something greater than themselves, motivation and commitment are naturally enhanced.

Personalizing Goals for Motivation

While the organizational vision provides the overarching direction, personalizing individual goals is essential to ignite motivation and create a sense of ownership. This involves:

Goal Customization

- Tailoring Objectives: Allowing team members a degree of autonomy in setting their individual goals tailors objectives to their strengths and preferences. This customization fosters a sense of ownership and personal investment.
- Empowering through Autonomy:** Empowering individuals to have a say in their goals enhances their sense of control, leading to increased motivation and a higher likelihood of goal achievement.

Recognizing Individual Strengths

- Strengths-Based Approach: Identifying and leveraging individual strengths when assigning goals ensures that tasks align with what team members excel at. This not only enhances performance but also boosts job satisfaction.
- Encouraging Growth: While capitalizing on strengths, leaders should encourage individuals to stretch beyond their comfort zones, fostering a growth mindset and continuous improvement.

Fostering a Growth Mindset

- Embracing Challenges: Encouraging a growth mindset involves viewing challenges not as obstacles but as opportunities for learning and development. Individuals with a growth mindset are more likely to embrace ambitious goals.
- Building Resilience: A growth mindset builds resilience, enabling team members to bounce back from setbacks and approach obstacles with a positive and adaptive attitude.

Connecting individual goals to the organizational vision is not just about alignment but about creating a narrative where each team member sees themselves as a vital contributor to the collective journey. This personalization not only enhances motivation but also ensures that individual efforts are channeled towards the realization of the broader organizational vision.

Reinforcing the Collective Vision

Creating a Shared Visionary Culture

To reinforce the collective vision, leaders need to foster a culture where the vision is not just a statement but an integral part of the team's identity. This involves:

Leadership Alignment

- Consistent Messaging: Ensuring that leaders at all levels are aligned with and consistently communicate the collective vision. Leadership alignment is essential to avoid confusion and maintain a unified focus.
- Leading by Example: Leaders should embody the values and behaviors associated with the vision. Their actions should reflect a commitment to the shared goals, serving as a model for the rest of the team.

Storytelling and Narratives

- Emotional Connection: Utilizing storytelling to communicate and reinforce the collective vision emotionally. Narratives create a connection between team members and the vision, making it more than a strategic goal but a shared journey.
- Anecdotes of Success: Sharing anecdotes of success and perseverance related to the collective vision inspires the team. Real stories of overcoming challenges build a sense of camaraderie and instill confidence in the shared vision.

Celebrating Achievements and Milestones
Recognizing and celebrating achievements that contribute to the collective vision is crucial for maintaining motivation and reinforcing commitment. This involves:

Recognition Programs
- Formal Acknowledgment: Implementing formal recognition programs that acknowledge outstanding contributions.

Publicly recognizing achievements reinforces the value of aligned efforts and motivates others to contribute similarly.

- Highlighting Team Success: Recognition should not solely focus on individual accomplishments but also highlight collaborative achievements that propel the team toward the collective vision.

Team-building Activities

- Fostering a Sense of Community: Incorporating team-building activities that strengthen the sense of community and shared purpose. These activities create bonds among team members, fostering collaboration in pursuit of the collective vision.

- Strategic Retreats and Workshops: Organizing strategic retreats or workshops that provide dedicated time for reflection on the collective vision. Such events create a space for deeper discussions and reinforce the importance of the shared journey.

Feedback Loops for Continuous Alignment

Establishing feedback mechanisms is vital to ensuring continuous alignment with the collective vision. This involves:

Regular Check-ins

- Open Communication: Channels Regular check-ins between team members and leaders ensure that communication channels remain open. This allows for ongoing alignment discussions and provides an opportunity to address any emerging challenges.
- Adaptability through Feedback: Creating a culture of adaptability by actively using feedback for continuous improvement. Regular check-ins not only serve as a platform for alignment but also contribute to the team's ability to adapt to changing circumstances.

Employee Surveys

- Insights into Team Dynamics: Conducting employee surveys to gather insights into team dynamics related to the collective vision. Feedback from team members provides valuable information for refining alignment strategies and addressing potential gaps.
- Incorporating Suggestions: Actively incorporating suggestions and concerns raised through employee surveys demonstrates a commitment to continuous improvement and ensures that the collective vision remains relevant.

Reinforcing the collective vision is an ongoing process that requires intentional effort and a commitment to nurturing a shared sense of purpose. By creating a culture where the vision is ingrained in daily operations, celebrating milestones, and incorporating feedback loops, leaders can ensure that the team remains aligned and inspired on its journey toward the collective vision.

CHAPTER FIVE

Transparency and Trust

Sharing Information Proactively

The Foundations of Transparency

In the realm of organizational dynamics, transparency acts as a cornerstone upon which trust is built. At its essence, transparency involves the deliberate and open sharing of information across all levels of an organization. The act of sharing information proactively transcends mere communication; it's a commitment to fostering an environment where knowledge is a shared asset, and every team member feels empowered by the information they possess.

The Value of Open Communication

Transparency is inherently linked to open communication, creating a workplace culture where information flows freely and is readily accessible. Leaders who prioritize open communication set the stage for a collaborative and informed team. This commitment has several notable values:

a. Fostering Collaboration

Proactive sharing of information cultivates an environment where collaboration thrives. Team members are equipped with the insights they need to contribute effectively, breaking down silos and promoting a collective approach to problem-solving.

b. Building Trust

Trust is nurtured when information is shared openly and consistently. Team members feel more secure in their roles and are more likely to trust leadership when they perceive that information is not being withheld or manipulated.

c. Enhancing Decision-Making

A well-informed team is better equipped to make informed decisions. By proactively sharing relevant information, leaders empower their teams to make decisions aligned with organizational goals, fostering a sense of ownership and responsibility.

Building a Foundation of Transparency

Transparency begins with leadership setting the tone. Leaders who prioritize transparency actively work to build a foundation grounded in open communication. This involves:

a. Setting Expectations

Leaders should set clear expectations regarding the importance of transparency. When openness is a stated value, team members understand the organizational culture that is expected.

b. Lead by Example

Leaders need to embody the transparency they advocate. When leaders model open communication by sharing information, admitting mistakes, and seeking input, they create a cultural precedent for the entire organization.

c. Encouraging Two-Way Communication

Effective transparency is not a one-way street. Leaders should encourage team members to share their thoughts, concerns, and ideas. This reciprocal communication reinforces a culture of openness.

Leveraging Technology for Transparency

In the digital age, technology plays a pivotal role in facilitating transparent communication. Leveraging tools and platforms for effective communication involves:

a. Collaboration Platforms

Utilizing collaboration platforms like Slack, Microsoft Teams, or other project management tools enhances real-time communication and document sharing, creating a centralized hub for information.

b. Data Visualization Tools

Using data visualization tools helps translate complex information into easily understandable formats. Visual aids enhance transparency by making data accessible and digestible.

c. Transparent Workflows

Implementing transparent workflows ensures that team members understand how tasks and projects progress. Tools that offer visibility into project timelines and milestones enhance clarity.

Case Studies: Successful Transparency Practices

Examining real-world case studies provides insights into successful transparency practices. Organizations that have excelled in this area often share common characteristics:

a. Google's Open Communication Culture

Google is renowned for its commitment to transparency. The company encourages employees to ask questions and provides forums where leadership addresses concerns openly. This practice contributes to a culture of trust and innovation.

b. Buffer's Radical Transparency

Buffer, a social media management platform, practices radical transparency by openly sharing its financial information, including salaries. This level of openness has fostered trust among employees and customers alike.

c. Zappos' Holacracy Implementation

Zappos, an online shoe retailer, embraced holacracy, a management philosophy that distributes authority. This shift towards a flatter organizational structure promotes transparency in decision-making and empowers employees at various levels.

Conclusion: The Ongoing Commitment to Transparency

In the intricate dance between transparency and trust, sharing information proactively is not a singular event but an ongoing commitment. Leaders must recognize that transparency is not about sharing only positive news but also addressing challenges openly. The act of sharing information proactively requires a dedication to creating an environment where information is not a currency hoarded by a few but a shared resource that propels the entire organization forward. As we delve deeper into the exploration of transparency and trust, the next focal point is on navigating difficult conversations effectively, a critical juncture where the fabric of trust is often tested and strengthened.

Navigating Difficult Conversations Effectively

The Crucial Role of Difficult Conversations

Navigating difficult conversations is an inevitable aspect of professional life, and the effectiveness with which these conversations are handled significantly influences the level of trust within an organization. This section explores how leaders can skillfully navigate challenging discussions, fostering an environment where trust is not only preserved but strengthened.

The Role of Difficult Conversations in Trust-Building

1. **Acknowledging Uncomfortable Realities**

   Difficult conversations often involve addressing uncomfortable truths or challenges. Leaders who acknowledge these realities openly demonstrate authenticity, a key element in building and maintaining trust.

   Avoiding difficult conversations can lead to unspoken tensions and erode trust over time.

2. **Opportunities for Growth**

   - Viewing difficult conversations as opportunities for growth reframes them from obstacles to chances for improvement. Leaders who convey this perspective foster a culture where challenges are met head-on and trust is built through shared problem-solving.

Communication Strategies for Difficult Conversations

1. Active Listening

Active listening is a cornerstone of effective communication during difficult conversations. Leaders should strive to understand the perspectives of others before formulating responses.

Creating an environment where team members feel heard contributes to a sense of respect and trust.

2. Empathy in Communication

Expressing empathy during difficult conversations involves acknowledging and validating others' emotions. Leaders who convey understanding and empathy build trust by demonstrating genuine concern for team members' experiences.

Connecting on an emotional level fosters a sense of camaraderie and shared humanity.

3. **Clarity in Conveying Difficult Messages**

Communicating difficult messages with clarity is essential. Leaders should strive to be transparent about the situation while providing context and explaining the rationale behind decisions.

Ambiguity or lack of clarity can create confusion and erode trust. Transparent communication, even when delivering challenging news, fosters a sense of honesty.

Conflict Resolution Techniques

1. **Mediation**

Mediation encompasses the involvement of a neutral third party guiding a conversation between conflicting parties, facilitating a resolution. This technique can be effective in resolving interpersonal conflicts and rebuilding trust.

An impartial mediator helps ensure that all perspectives are considered, fostering a fair resolution.

2. Negotiation

Negotiation is a collaborative approach to conflict resolution. Leaders should encourage open dialogue, compromise, and finding common ground.

A negotiated resolution allows team members to feel heard and actively involved in finding solutions, promoting trust in the decision-making process.

3. Collaborative Problem-Solving

Approaching difficult conversations as opportunities for collaborative problem-solving shifts the focus from blame to solutions. Leaders should encourage team members to work together to address challenges.

Teams that collectively find solutions during difficult conversations build trust through shared responsibility for outcomes.

Leadership Presence in Difficult Moments

1. Maintaining Composure

Leaders must maintain composure during difficult conversations. Emotional intelligence plays a crucial role in managing one's emotions while addressing challenging issues.

Demonstrating emotional resilience fosters trust, as team members look to leaders for stability and guidance in challenging moments.

2. Empathy in Leadership Presence

Leadership presence during difficult moments requires a genuine display of empathy. Leaders should not only understand but also convey empathy for the emotional impact of challenging situations on team members.

Leaders who empathize build stronger connections and trust with their teams.

Case Studies: Navigating Difficult Conversations Successfully

1. IBM's Cultural Transformation

IBM faced the challenge of transforming its culture during times of significant change. Open and transparent communication about the need for change, coupled with active listening to employee concerns, facilitated a successful cultural shift.

2. Starbucks' Response to Racial Bias

Starbucks navigated a difficult conversation on racial bias by closing its stores for a day of training. The company openly acknowledged the issue, engaged in active listening, and took tangible steps to address the concerns raised by the community.

3. Microsoft's Shift in Organizational Structure

Microsoft underwent a major organizational restructuring. Transparent communication from leadership about the reasons behind the changes, coupled with empathy for employees affected, contributed to a smoother transition and maintained trust within the organization.

Conclusion: The Transformative Power of Difficult Conversations

In conclusion, the art of navigating difficult conversations is transformative for trust-building within an organization. Leaders who embrace these challenging moments as opportunities for growth, employ effective communication strategies, leverage conflict resolution techniques, and maintain a strong leadership presence contribute to an environment where trust not only endures challenges but emerges stronger. The next segment delves into the proactive implementation of trust-building strategies, exploring how organizations can embed trust into their core values and daily operations.

Implementing Trust-Building Strategies

Foundations of Trust

1. Defining Trust in the Organizational Context

Trust is a multifaceted concept within organizations, encompassing reliability, integrity, and openness. Defining trust lays the groundwork for developing targeted strategies.

Leaders must articulate a clear understanding of what trust means within the specific context of their organization.

2. The Interplay Between Trust and Organizational Culture

Trust is deeply interwoven with organizational culture. Leaders should actively shape a culture that encourages trust-building behaviors.

A culture of openness, accountability, and ethical conduct creates an environment where trust can flourish.

Leadership Trustworthiness

1. Consistency in Actions and Words

Trustworthy leadership is characterized by consistency between words and actions. Leaders who align their behaviors with stated values build credibility.

Inconsistencies erode trust, emphasizing the importance of leaders being true to their commitments.

2. **Transparency as a Leadership Practice**
   Transparent leadership practices, where leaders openly share information about decisions and strategies, contribute to trustworthiness.

When leaders communicate openly, team members are more likely to perceive them as trustworthy and credible.

Cultivating a Culture of Trust

1. **Encouraging Open Communication**
   Cultivating a culture of trust requires an environment where open communication is not only encouraged but celebrated.

Leaders should create channels for team members to express opinions, share feedback, and ask questions without fear of reprisal.

2. Building Psychological Safety

Psychological safety is fundamental to trust. Leaders must foster an atmosphere where team members feel safe to take risks, share ideas, and admit mistakes.

Establishing psychological safety promotes a culture of trust where innovation and collaboration thrive.

Continuous Evaluation and Improvement

1. Feedback Mechanisms for Trust Assessment

Implementing regular feedback mechanisms allows organizations to assess the level of trust within teams and the broader organization.

Anonymous surveys, town hall meetings, and one-on-one discussions provide valuable insights into trust perceptions.

2. Addressing Trust Gaps Promptly

When trust gaps are identified, prompt action is essential. Leaders should address concerns transparently, sharing plans for improvement.

Demonstrating a commitment to addressing trust issues reinforces the organization's dedication to continuous improvement.

Case Studies: Exemplary Trust-Building Organizations

1. Patagonia's Ethical Business Practices

Patagonia, a company committed to ethical and sustainable business practices, has built trust with its customers through transparency about its supply chain, environmental initiatives, and fair labor practices.

2. Toyota's Emphasis on Continuous Improvement

Toyota's success is attributed in part to its dedication to continuous improvement, a principle deeply rooted in trust-building. Open communication and a commitment to addressing issues as they arise contribute to a culture of trust.

3. Southwest Airlines' Employee-Centric Approach

Southwest Airlines has fostered a culture of trust by prioritizing its employees. Open communication channels, a commitment to work-life balance, and a focus on employee well-being contribute to a high level of trust within the organization.

Conclusion: Embedding Trust in Organizational DNA

In conclusion, implementing trust-building strategies involves a holistic approach that encompasses leadership trustworthiness, organizational culture, and continuous improvement. Trust is not a static entity but a dynamic force that requires consistent attention and intentional efforts. By cultivating an environment where trust is embedded in the organizational DNA, leaders pave the way for sustained success, employee satisfaction, and long-term positive relationships. The journey towards transparency and trust is an ongoing process, and organizations that embrace this journey are better positioned to navigate challenges and thrive in a rapidly evolving business landscape.

CHAPTER 6

Sustainable Leadership Practices

The Essence of Sustainable Leadership

Defining Sustainable Leadership

In the ever-evolving landscape of leadership, the concept of sustainable leadership has emerged as a guiding philosophy that transcends traditional approaches. Sustainable leadership is not merely about achieving short-term goals or maximizing immediate profits; rather, it embodies a holistic and forward-thinking mindset. At its core, sustainable leadership seeks a harmonious balance between the well-being of people, the preservation of the planet, and the pursuit of long-term economic prosperity. It's a visionary approach that goes beyond the constraints of quarterly reports, envisioning a future where leadership practices contribute to a thriving ecosystem for all stakeholders.

The Importance of Long-term Impact

Sustainable leadership recognizes that the impact of leadership decisions extends far beyond the confines of the present moment. While short-term gains may be appealing, a sustainable leader understands the imperative of considering the enduring consequences of their actions. This involves strategic planning that looks beyond immediate challenges and envisions a trajectory that ensures the organization's resilience, adaptability, and success in the long run. By prioritizing long-term impact, sustainable leaders lay the groundwork for an organizational legacy that transcends their tenure.

Balancing People, Planet, and Profit

In the pursuit of sustainability, a delicate equilibrium must be maintained between the well-being of individuals, the health of the planet, and the financial prosperity of the organization. Sustainable leaders recognize that these elements are interconnected and interdependent. A focus on people involves empowering and nurturing the talents of individuals, fostering a workplace culture that values diversity, equity, and inclusion. Simultaneously, a commitment to the planet entails responsible environmental stewardship, acknowledging the impact of organizational practices on the broader ecosystem. Finally, sustaining profitability is not an end in itself but a means to ensure the continued positive impact of the organization.

As we embark on this exploration of sustainable leadership practices, it is essential to appreciate the transformative potential that lies within this paradigm. Sustainable leadership is not a singular trait or a fixed set of practices but a dynamic and evolving approach that responds to the complexities of our interconnected world. Throughout this chapter, we will delve into the core elements of sustainable leadership: empowering others in leadership roles, focusing on long-term success strategies, and leaving a lasting positive impact. Each aspect contributes to the broader tapestry of sustainable leadership, weaving together a narrative of responsible, visionary, and impactful leadership practices.

Empowering Others in Leadership Roles

The Collaborative Leadership Model

1. Delegating with Purpose

Empowering others in leadership roles begins with a purposeful approach to delegation. Sustainable leaders understand that distributing responsibilities is not merely a task but a strategic investment in building a robust and adaptive organizational structure. Delegating with clarity and purpose involves not only assigning tasks but also communicating the significance of each role within the broader context of the organization's mission. This approach fosters a sense of ownership, where individuals see their contributions as integral to the collective success.

2. Nurturing Leadership Skills in Others

The essence of sustainable leadership lies in nurturing the leadership potential within each team member. Leaders who empower others recognize that leadership is not confined to a select few but is a collective force that can be cultivated. This involves creating an environment where individuals are encouraged to develop and showcase their leadership skills. Mentoring and coaching become vital tools in the sustainable leader's toolkit, providing guidance and support to individuals as they navigate their own leadership journeys.

Inclusive Decision-Making

1. Diversity in Leadership

Empowerment reaches its zenith when leadership is diverse and inclusive. Sustainable leaders champion diversity not just as a checkbox but as an integral component that enhances decision-making. This involves breaking down traditional hierarchies and welcoming individuals from varied backgrounds, experiences, and perspectives into leadership roles. The result is a rich tapestry of ideas and approaches that contribute to more innovative and sustainable solutions.

2. Collaborative Decision-Making

In the realm of sustainable leadership, decisions are not imposed from the top down but crafted collaboratively. Empowering others in leadership involves a participatory approach to decision-making where team members are active contributors. Sustainable leaders recognize that collective intelligence far surpasses individual brilliance. Engaging in open dialogues, brainstorming sessions, and fostering a culture where ideas are valued, regardless of hierarchy, leads to decisions that are not only sustainable but resonate with the entire team.

Continuous Learning and Development

1. Promoting a Learning Culture

Sustainable leaders understand that empowerment is an ongoing process intertwined with continuous learning. Organizations that prioritize a learning culture invest in the professional and personal development of their team members. This involves providing access to learning resources, workshops, and encouraging pursuits that expand the skill set of individuals. By promoting a learning culture, sustainable leaders ensure that team members are equipped to embrace leadership roles with confidence and competence.

2. Feedback as a Tool for Growth

In the realm of sustainable leadership, feedback is not a one-time event but an integral component of the empowerment journey. Leaders provide constructive feedback that serves as a catalyst for growth. This involves creating a feedback loop where individuals are not only evaluated but also encouraged to provide feedback upward and sideways. Sustainable leaders recognize that the growth of individuals directly contributes to the overall sustainability of the organization.

Empowering others in leadership roles is not a passive act but an intentional and dynamic process that aligns with the principles of sustainability. Sustainable leaders understand that the strength of an organization lies not just in the leadership at the top but in the collective leadership potential distributed across the entire team. As we explore the facets of sustainable leadership, this commitment to empowerment becomes a cornerstone, shaping an organizational culture that thrives on collaboration, diversity, and continuous growth.

Focusing on Long-term Success Strategies

Strategic Vision and Planning

1. Defining Organizational Purpose

Long-term success strategies commence with a clear definition of organizational purpose. Sustainable leaders guide their organizations beyond profit-centric motives, emphasizing a broader sense of purpose that aligns with societal and environmental values. Defining purpose provides a guiding light, shaping strategic decisions and fostering a collective understanding of the organization's contribution to a sustainable future.

2. Strategic Planning for Sustainability

Sustainable leaders recognize that strategic planning is not solely about immediate gains but about charting a course for enduring success. Long-term success strategies incorporate sustainability as a central theme. This involves a comprehensive examination of environmental, social, and economic impacts. By embedding sustainability into strategic plans, organizations position themselves to weather changes, adapt to evolving market dynamics, and contribute positively to the well-being of the planet and society.

Environmental and Social Responsibility

1. Corporate Social Responsibility (CSR)

Long-term success goes hand-in-hand with a robust commitment to Corporate Social Responsibility (CSR). Sustainable leaders view CSR not as a compliance checkbox but as a genuine dedication to making a positive impact on society. Initiatives that address environmental concerns, support social causes, and enhance community well-being become integral components of an organization's identity and contribute to sustained success.

2. Ethical Leadership Practices

Ethical leadership is foundational to long-term success. Sustainable leaders prioritize ethical decision-making, ensuring that organizational actions align with values, principles, and societal expectations. By adopting ethical practices, leaders build trust with stakeholders, fortify the organizational reputation, and lay the groundwork for enduring success that transcends market fluctuations.

Adaptability and Resilience

1. Agile Leadership

In a rapidly changing world, sustainable leaders embrace agile leadership principles. This involves the ability to pivot and adapt swiftly to unforeseen circumstances. Agile leaders cultivate organizational cultures that value flexibility, innovation, and the capacity to navigate uncertainties, positioning the organization for sustained success in an ever-evolving landscape.

2. Future-proofing Strategies

Sustainable leaders engage in future-proofing by anticipating and preparing for emerging trends and challenges. This strategic foresight involves staying ahead of technological advancements, market shifts, and societal changes. Organizations that implement future-proofing strategies position themselves as leaders rather than followers, contributing to sustained success in a dynamic and unpredictable global environment.

Long-term success strategies in sustainable leadership extend beyond quarterly performance indicators. Sustainable leaders recognize that success is not solely measured by financial metrics but by the lasting positive impact an organization has on the world. As we delve deeper into sustainable leadership practices, the focus on long-term success strategies becomes a compass guiding organizations towards resilience, relevance, and a legacy that extends far beyond the present moment.

Leaving a Lasting Positive Impact

Leadership Legacy

1. Defining Leadership Legacy

Sustainable leaders understand that their impact extends beyond their immediate tenure. Defining a leadership legacy involves reflecting on the mark one wishes to leave on the organization, its people, and the broader world. It transcends personal achievements and emphasizes the enduring values and principles that will continue to guide the organization long after a leader has moved on.

2. Succession Planning with Impact

Succession planning becomes a strategic element in sustainable leadership. It involves identifying and nurturing individuals who not only possess the requisite skills for leadership roles but also align with the organization's sustainable values. Sustainable leaders ensure a smooth transition by imparting their knowledge, values, and insights to the next generation of leaders, ensuring the organization's sustainability journey remains uninterrupted.

Community and Global Impact

1. Engaging with the Community

Sustainable leaders recognize the interconnectedness between their organizations and the communities they serve. Engaging with the community involves more than philanthropy; it requires active participation, understanding local needs, and contributing meaningfully to community development. By fostering positive relationships with the community, sustainable leaders ensure that their organizations are viewed not as outsiders but as integral parts of a larger societal ecosystem.

2. Global Responsibility

In the era of globalization, sustainable leaders acknowledge their organizations' global impact. Global responsibility entails more than just complying with international standards; it involves proactively addressing global challenges. Sustainable leaders collaborate on a global scale, sharing best practices, contributing to sustainable development goals, and ensuring that their organizations are not just global players but responsible global citizens.

Conclusion: Nurturing Sustainable Leadership in Every Sphere

As we conclude the exploration of leaving a lasting positive impact in sustainable leadership, it becomes evident that sustainable leaders view their roles as stewards of not only organizational success but also societal and environmental well-being. The commitment to a positive legacy, thoughtful succession planning, and active community and global engagement are not optional add-ons; they are integral components of a leadership philosophy that seeks to leave the world in a better state than it was found.

The principles uncovered in this chapter—empowering others in leadership roles, focusing on long-term success strategies, and leaving a lasting positive impact—are not isolated practices but interconnected threads that weave together a tapestry of sustainable leadership. As organizations and leaders embrace these principles, they not only secure their own longevity but contribute meaningfully to the broader narrative of building a sustainable and thriving future for all.